MAGUA AND THE MONSTER BLADE MASTERS

Journal of Lithic Research
Vol. 4

By Ray Harwood

Published by Spokane River Trading Company
2020 Copyright

Permissive use was obtained for all content

ISBN – see back cover

PRINTED IN THE UNITED STATES OF AMERICA
10 9 8 7 6 5 4 3 2 1
First Edition

WARNING:
Flintknapping is very dangerous and can cause, severe
lacerations, silicosis and many other serious health
Problems; including death.
If you do so it is only at your own risk.

Front cover and blade art by Val Waldorf; Crows' Nest Studio
thank you to the PSK.

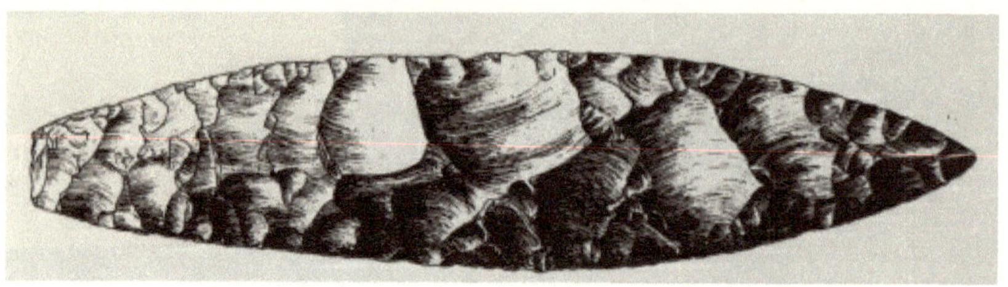

PSK. KNAPPERS' CODE OF ETHICS:
The Puget Sound Knappers will not condone, encourage or sanc-
tion the following activities:
The sale of prehistoric artifacts.
Alteration of prehistoric sites.
Sale of modern replicas as authentic prehistoric artifacts.
The sale of modern replicas which do not clearly display perman-
ent marks to distinguish the replicas as modern.
The leaving of a knapping area without policing the debitage,
dating and burying it with coins, cans, etc.
Digging or collecting artifacts in a known prehistoric site.

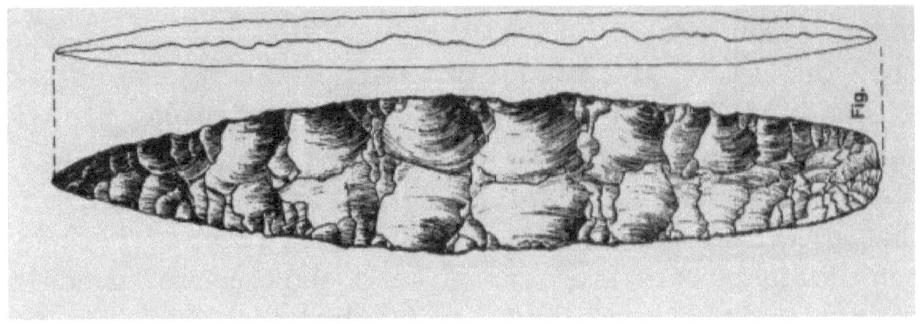

What is flintknapping? Flintknapping is described as the art of making stone tools, such as arrowheads, knife blades, spear points, atlatl points, scrapers, etc., by removing flakes from glass-like or flint-like, stone via percussion or pressure flaking methods. Two major concepts known as modes are in play 1) preparation mode, knapping done to prepare a surface for flake removal; i.e. abrading, shearing, platform setup, platform preparation and alternate flaking. 2) The second concept is reduction mode knapping, this fallows up each individual preparation mode segment with applied preconceived and calculated applied energy, in the form of pressure or impact. Combining these two modes systematically and sequentially is the attack, or battle plan, in the reduction of the mass of 3 dimensional stone to a flat, 2 dimensional, form. Mode 1 and mode 2 are alternated like Karate; block and then kick and block and then punch, block and two finger eye poke and so on.

My wilderness survival expert friend, Joe Dabil, described knapping best; "Knock a long flake of proper thickness from a core of obsidian or flint, abrade the edges to strengthen and dull them, then alternate flake the edge into a margin of well-spaced platforms and press the tip of an antler against the platforms until the flakes come off in a bifacial flaked arrowhead shape, with a lens shaped cross section, then put notches into the lower base area and tie it to a stick.

The word "knap," of Germanic or Gaelic origin, means to break with a quick blow or to shape by breaking off pieces. In 18th and 19th century England, a flint knapper was a skilled craftsman who chipped gunflints for flintlock firearms. It sounds better than arrowhead chipper, some knappers are in need of the fancy name for many of their egos are gigantic, and they are legends in their own mind. Flint knapping is one of humans oldest crafts, no matter what your heritage is, your ancestors flint-knapped. Like fire building and wood working, flintknapping is etched into our DNA as one of our basic human survival skill. The oldest known stone tools, found by archaeologists, were discovered at sites in the Olduvai Gorge of East Africa, these unearthed by my childhood hero, Dr. Luis Leaky, some date back millions of years. The Olduvai Gorge in Tanzania is one of the most important paleo-anthropological and early stone tool sites in the world. Dr. Leaky learned early the knowledge of primitive skills, including flint working. Dr. Leakey went to Cambridge University, majoring in anthropology. Leaky landed a job on an international archaeological mission to Tanzania as soon as he graduated college. During WWII Leaky was a spy posing as an archaeologist. It was 1949 when Leaky discovered the first Proconsul skull, a missing link. Dr. Leaky did many television specials for National Geographic and often including flintknapping and experimental use of the stone tools. Leaky conducted many flintknapping demonstrations showing how stone tool making developed in conjunction with the human brain and culture its self. The act of flintlnapping is a rather moderately entertaining past-time, but it can take you on a world of adventure.

Accoring to the Puget Sound Knappers, the largest of the knapper club, flintknapping is defined as the art of making stone tools such as arrowheads, knife blades, spear points, atlatl points, scrapers, etc., by remove flakes from conchoidal stone via percussion or pressure flaking. The "dean of American flintknapping", Don Crabtree defined a flintknapper as one who forms stone implements by controlling the fracture of the material. A knapper is an artificer or a stoneworker using conchoidal fracture. Obsidian bearing well-developed conchoidal (clam-shell-shaped, conch sea shell) fracture with concentric rings, like when you through a rock into still water. A common "bb" hole "cone" fracture in glass is a complete fracture as a conchoidal spall (flake) would be a partial cone. The cone that pops out of the opposite side of the glass from the entry hole of the bb is called the "Hertzian" cone or Hertzian fracture. This phenomenon is named for a German physicist named Heinrich Rudolf Hertz whom studied the "bb" hole in detail.

Don E. Crabtree is often referred to as the "Dean of American Flintknapping". He was awarded an honorary doctorate degree from the University of Idaho for his outstanding contributions in the field of experimental archaeology. His 1972 publication entitled An Introduction to Flintworking is still one of the primary sources for students of lithic technology. Through practical experimentation, along with the study of stone tools and manufacturing debris found in the archaeological record, Don Crabtree was able to produce exact replicas of various ancient blades. His famous "Crabtree's Law," states that; "the greater degree of final finish applied to a stone artifact, whether by flaking, grinding, and/or polishing, the harder it is to conclude the lithic reduction process which produced the stone artifact. Crabtree had classes on flintknapping in the early 1970s but they were hard to get in.

The cone is the essential component of flintknapping, "termed lithic technology" by and in the Crabtree era academic world, because every flake starts with that cone. The flakes are detached with either a "percussion flaking" blow, to a prepared or natural platform, with a hammer-stone or pressed of with "pressure flaking" from a pressure flaking tool. An indirect percussion method is similar to chiseling with a hammer and chisel. Pressure flaking is the shaping by removing, or chipping off sequential flakes.

Large stone artifacts or modern knapped pieces are known as bifaces, and the act of knapping them is known as "bifacing". Biface simply means chipped on both sides, you must have the flakes cover the entire faces or you are doomed to social criticism. The biface (two faced) artifact is thinned, by flaking, into a lens or platter shape cross section, when viewed from the tip or base with flake scars on both top and bottom faces. Lithic is the term referring to flint-like or class-like stone used for chipped stone-age technology. Stone bowls or axes are not considered lithic. Arrowheads, flint knives, flint spear points are examples of biface lithic technology. Usually ovoid bifacially flaked blades are called bifaces, width to thickness ratio on this type artifact is a major status issue in all known flintknapping communities, both past and present. A biface in the knap-in vernacular would usually refer to direct percussion artifacts, usually over 5 inches long and three inches wide and above. "To biface" is to sit on a stump or stool and thin, with soft hammer percussion, reduce a large lithic spall into a bifacially flaked perform. "The Sweet Water Biface" is the ultimate representation of this artifact and knapping technique. The extraordinary Sweetwater biface was in the artifact collection of the late Charlie Shewey, it was found by a Mr. Roland Kamer from Sweetwater, Texas. The blade was found while Kramer was hunting rattlesnakes in 1986. The Sweet Water biface could be related to the ancient group of Indians known as the Caddoan Culture and Harahey Knives. The date of these master biface knappers were around A.D. 1300 to A.D. 1500. It was probably used as a knife for butchering and killing, butchering and skinning game animals, used in hand to hand close in combat with enemies, a ceremonial object or grave goods. I have a cast of it I purchased from Peter Bostrom's Casting Lab, it is wonderful! The wider the biface is, the harder it is to strike off large thinning flakes across the midline of the flaked surfaces, in order to thin down the cross-section without breaking it. The Sweetwater Biface measures 9 7/16 inches long and 3 3/8 inches wide, and 3/16 of an inch thick. Thickness ranges down to 1/16 width thickness ratio. I found one in Emory's waste pile that was equally impressive that he had simply tossed aside.

Unfortunately flintknapping is used by some unscrupulous individuals to create fraudulent artifacts, but most knappers sell what they create as art, or use it as a vital tool in the study of ancient flaked stone artifacts, again this science known as "lithic technology". Lithic Technology is essentially experimental flintknapping; tool production, use, and maintenance and subsequent analysis.

According to the John Whitaker, an archaeologist and accomplished flintknapper, in an article he penned in1998 for American Antiquity, at the time of his research; the average knapper makes about 25 flint arrow points per month. The article estimated there were 5,000 active knappers. Calculating the 25 newly knapped points a day with the 5,000 active knappers, this would be in the neighborhood of 1.5 million modern flint points per year.

Below is the famous and very thin and well flaked, Sweet Water Biface.

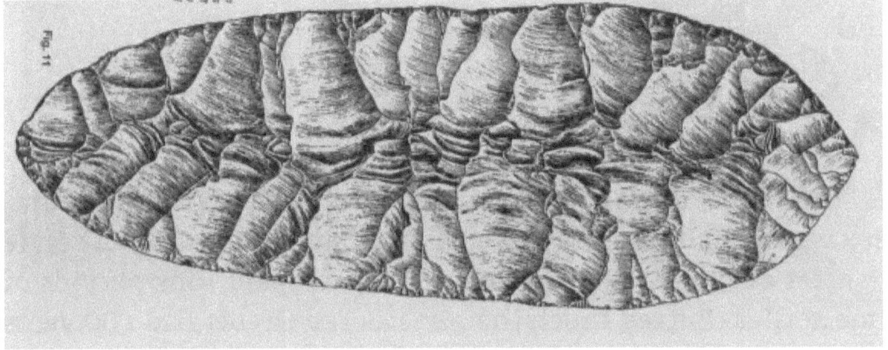

Blade Art: Val Waldorf, Crows' Nest Art Studio: "The Sweet Water"

M ike Tylznski (Magua) is considered by most to be the premiere flintknapper in Idaho, having mastered very high levels of competency in all of the extremely complex varied technologies. Mike has mastered the Ted Orcutt style monster obsidian wealth blades. Mike has spent long periods of time at Glass Buttes, much the same as Ted Orcutt had 100 years before; Mike also knaps giants Clovis type fluted paleo points.

Mike Tylznski is familiar with the many various types of obsidian in the Northwest. He trained quite extensively with knapping
icon Greg Ratzat of "Neolithics" knapping company. "Neolithics"
is a company that deals with top of the line lithic material to

customers from all over the world. Mr. Ratzat has participated in t research of obsidian blades for surgical scalpels, for science experiments and for display in prestigious museums and galleries. Along with numerous awards for excellence, artisan Craig Ratzat has established a place in the flintknappers's "Hall of Fame". His fascination with this art form has spanned a period of approximately fifty years. The number and expertise of the Neolithic students including, but not limited too; Mike Tylznski, Grog Verbeck and Gary Picket, all showcased in this publication, which attended Craig's school, is a testament to his professionalism and expertise. Neolithics has also produced a DVD knapping classes for those of us that have not been able to attend the school.

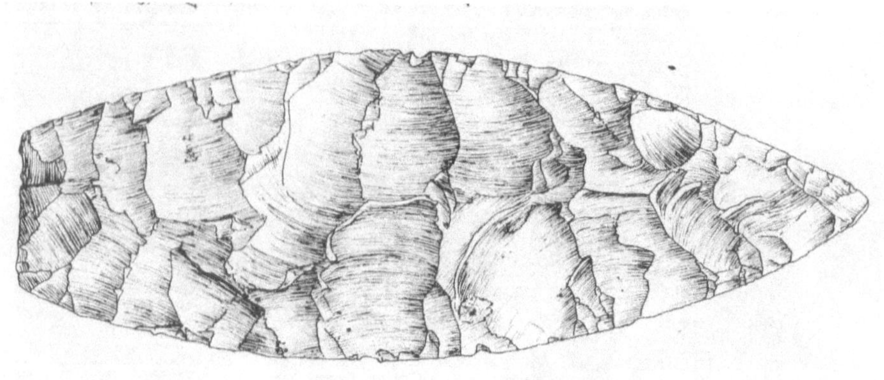

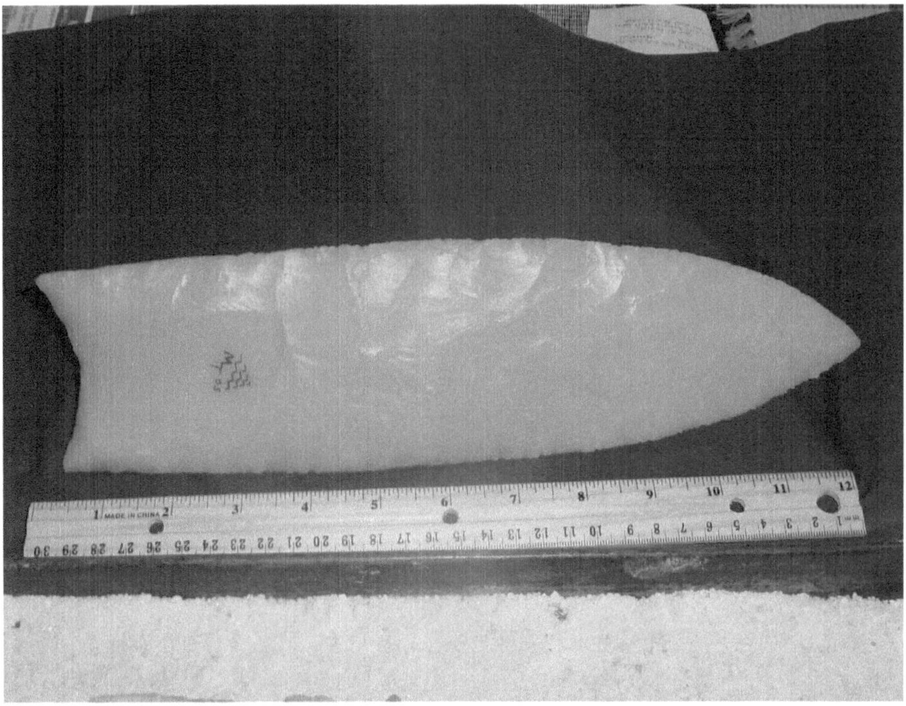

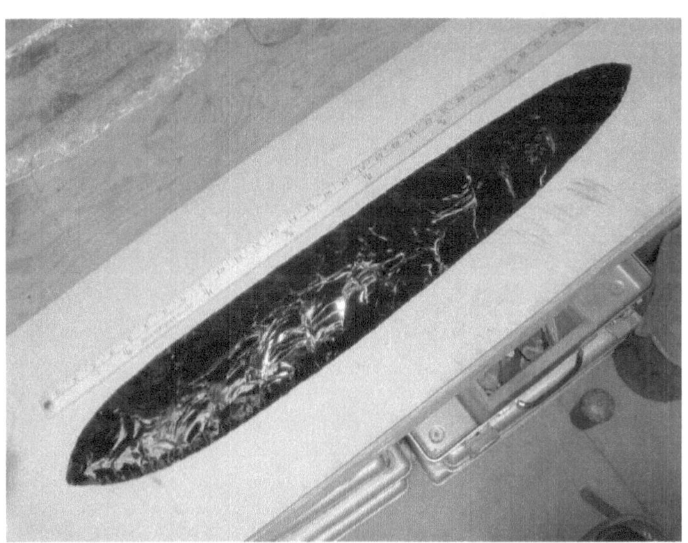

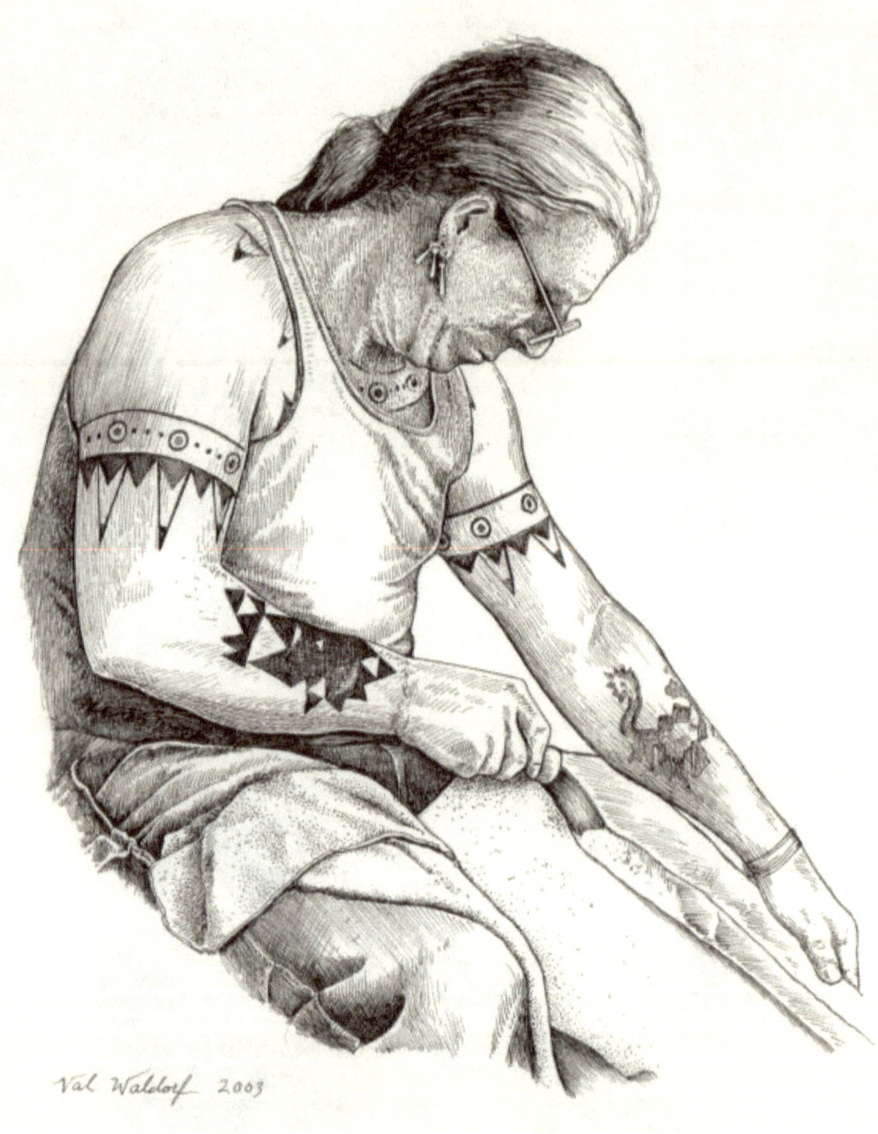

It all began at the age of six when finding an arrowhead in his parent's garden. It was the start of a long journey that took him from terrorizing his sisters with makeshift bow and arrow to working with some of the best teachers of flint knapping available. Craig is now one of those teachers himself. He has produced two very successful DVD's and teaches workshops throughout the year." Mike Tylzynski "Magua" lives in Central Idaho. He's part of the Lithic Artists Society, dedicated to preserving the ancient art of flintknapping. Mike has been able to make a living by "the way of the stone" for many years and is considered among the few true "masters".

Mike Tylzynski, formally of Rathdrum, Idaho now lives on the Nez Perce Indian Reservation near Lenore, Idaho. He has been flintknapping for about 20 years, he was lucky, in the time he learned how to knap, the Glass Buttes, Oregon, the largest obsidian outcrop, was open to large limits of stone than it is today and Mike was able to obtain massive amounts of obsidian

and practice, knapping 8 hours a day, and did so for almost three years. Having that much material played a huge part in how fast he learned and in the huge size of the blades he knapped. Again, most of Mike's formal instruction came from flintknapper, Craig Ratzat of Oregon. Craig Ratzat is considered a pivotal character in the history of modern flintknapping history.

"I think I went to the Graig Ratzat School for 9 years in a row, all the while looking for ever bigger and better pieces of Obsidian to knap into large mega blades." says Mike. Once the proper techniques are learned and muscle memory intact, the limiting component on Mike's large dance blades was, and especially is, obtaining a large enough, crack free,

piece of lithic material. Now with the unreasonably small weight limits put on obsidian collecting at the Glass Buttes, it has become nearly impossible to obtain large specimens of raw material. According to Mike Tylzynski; "flintknapping a very large blade (over 30 inches) is a extremely arduous task, and not for the faint of heart, even a slab that long will physically and mentally, wear you out with the constant turning and lifting of the heavy and sharp preform, over and over, so Mike always worked in 2 hour segments, that was about all a person can take before getting fatigued and large blades and tired do not mix, one wrong lazy hit and you have two small blades and that piece of rare material is gone forever" so, the key is work smart be aggressive, and have tons of patience. My style of knapping large blades is all done in my lap and with the slab laying down my leg and resting on my foot, sometimes I even padded my foot to dampen the blows, it is imperative you take large flakes so every blow counts you only get so many hits on a large blade. Support is what it is all about you have to support both the ends and the middle on each and every blow or again you will end up with two or four or more" At 69 years old now Mike's eyes are starting to weaken and it is having an a effect on his knapping.

Mike has slowed down and does not flintknap as often as he used to, but like an old surfer looking for that last set of huge waves, or an old prospector seeking that last big gold nugget, Mike still keeps a keen eye out for that last giant Obsidian boulder and his ultimate masterpiece. "It doesn't matter if you're white, black or red, your ancestors made stone tools," he said. "You wouldn't be here without them."

(Photos curtesy of Mike Tylznski, Magwa)

 "I never had any sister's, only one brother and as a child I terrorized everyone equally! Lol, my nick name Magua, actually came from a guy called Doc Ivory he is a dentist and a member of the American mountain men. That nick name came from the book "Last of the Mohicans" I have always loved elk and mule deer hunting and I fish over 100 days a year. Now that the mountains are getting taller so I fish more and I took my last elk 2 years ago, my 39th elk ,maybe I will get another but if not I am ok with it. I still love knapping and visiting with other knappers, but arthritis and poor eyes have a way of slowing me down Lol.   Now days I like to keep a good garden and enjoy the grandkids, the flint knapping world has been very good to me and I thank each and every person who helped me on this journey.

Gary Pickett is another Graig Ratzat student and knapper of large percussion obsidian blades. Gary has spent most of his life banging rocks together, and he's gotten rather good at it. The former President of the Kern County Archeological Society is well known throughout the western states for his beautiful creations and his knowledge of and respect for the ancient methods that render stone into objects of function and intricate form. Gary has a great respect for Ted Orcutt and the tradition of wealth blades and their ceremonial significance. Gary has been a friend of mine for many years; I have attended many knap-ins, pow-wows, rock shows and more. He has a high degree of integrity; he donates all his giant blades to the Indians to auction off at pow-wows. Some of the rainbow obsidian ones, knapped from giant slabs, sold for 800 to 1,000 dollars each.

What Gary is likely best known for is his willingness to teach and share the ancient art of flintknapping, and he'll be doing those week-ends, all over California and often at knap-ins, powwows, demonstrations. Gary and myself started and hosted the Bakersfield knap-n, world's longest running monthly knap in which started September 1999 and continues, this it's forth decade 248 knap-in and counting. His longest obsidian biface was 22 inches and 6 inches wide and under an inch thick, an impressive for the mass at 6/1 in width thickness ratio. The key elements are platform prep and support. The flipping of the heavy obsidian biface, over and over again, while knapping it, was tedious. The immense Glass Buttes obsidian biface had the weight of 22 pounds "that was a work out". I use various sizes copper stock in my percussion knapping. Mr. Pickett uses the D.C. Waldorf, they are both from Missouri, work bench method for Pressure flaking and uses an antler time pressure flaker. His Bakersfield friend Patrick Aims, a fellow Craig Ratzat student, built him a portable knapping bench for knap-ins and pow-wows. I had the pleasure of making several knapping videos of Gary working some large slabs he procured from Neolithics.

.Peter Wayne Ainsworth 1955 ~ 2009 Peter Wayne Ainsworth. Peter was born April 10, 1955 in Bethesda, Maryland while his father was serving in the U.S. Marine Corps. He was the oldest of three children of Marvin and Aline Ainsworth, and grew up in San Diego, California. He graduated from University High School in San Diego in 1973 and served in the U.S. Marine Corps between 1977 and 1979.He would joke about my career in the Marine Corps, it lasted 3 days and I washed out of flight school and later went into the Army instead. He received his B.A. and M.A. in Anthropology from the University of Utah and lived with his wife Betsy in Salt Lake City, Utah for the last 13 years of his life. Peter's lifelong passion was archaeology and primitive technology. Peter was a good friend and we had many a fun camp out and knap-in adventures. He would show up and knap-ins with his wife Betsy Skinner and his friend and fellow Don Crabtree student, Jeannie Binning. He had attended the Crabtree School and that of Jeff Flenniken. I remember discussing his studies in crescent flakes from notching found at archaeological sites and knapping big bifaces. Peter made me a 29 inch long and 6 inch wide biface out of Glass Buttes obsidian blade in 1985, he took it to show a fellow knapper and I never saw it again. He was a traditional knapper.

Jim Winn, while Jim did not want to provide information on his knapping career, I needed to convey what little I know about him. I met him in 1985 and visited and knapped with him at knap-ins every year for most of my life. He started making big blades

after meeting Emory Coons in the 1980s. He had a massive fal-
lowing on his knapping YouTube channel and has mastered all
known knapping styles. He was quite abrasive with me socially,
so I never really got to know him. He was in upper management
with a water reclamation center and retired to the desert of Nevada to pursue meteorite hunting. He has sold off his enormous
lithic supply, tools and lithic art. He was a true master knapper.
I recall going on one flint hunt with him to the "Peanut butter"
flint source in the Mojave desert, and hunting with our atlatls and
bows in the hills outside the San Fernando Valley of California.
We fluted our first points together at his condo in the valley in 85.
He knapped many big blades out of dacite and basidian.

Ray Harwood, My own experience with giant blades, is three-fold, the largest percussion bifaces I have knapped were 16 inches long and 8 inches wide, these were made of Glass Buttes silver sheen obsidian and knapped with traditional tools, no copper or saw. The longest blades I made, with the pressure method, were flaked points I made from the Northridge earthquake store front glass. These were pressure flaked swords from 18 to 29 inches long and only 1 to 3 inches wide and ¼ inch thick. All knapped by hand with an Ishi stick with a copper tip, a rubber slotted block and a chunk of grinding wheel for abrading. Then there was my lever flaked monster bifaces knapped blades that where 24 to 45 inches long and 4 inches wide. I learned how to lever flake by reading about Bryan Rinehart, a famous Texas knapper, known for inventing lapidary-slab and lever flaking techniques, and a California knapper named Robert Blue, whom set me up with my lever flaking rig. The photo on the next page is of me in my squatch hunting shirt holding one of over 100 giant lever flaked points I produced. Although my fellow flintknappers have given me nothing but insults on my giant blades, the archaeology community, gem and mineral community and general public rave about them. I have crafted them out of everything from table top glass to silica-infused mudstone to Glass Buttes obsidians. Many are in private collections of millionaires, elites and various museums around the globe. The lever only works on the face; alternate flaking with a indirect percussion and Ishi stick is required to finish up the job

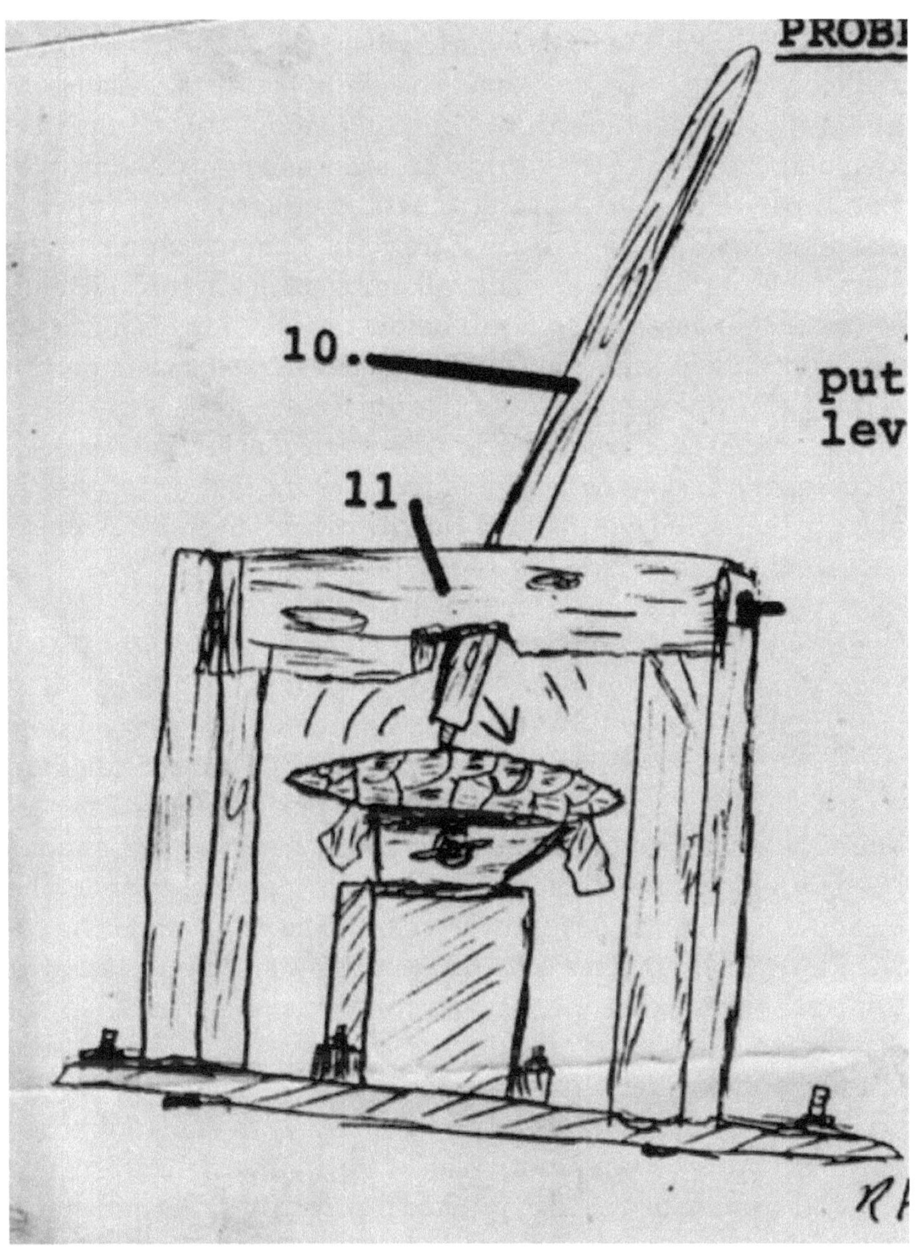

Here I am knapping a bifaced blade in the woods of the northwest;
I put the Karuk Indian word where I could, this to honor Ted Orcutt. While many knap for a source of income, to me flintknapping is like a time machine, it takes me back into another time or

dimeson. It takes me to the world where the smell of camp fire and clouds white sage smoke fill the air. In the distance a dream like drone of a deer hide drum, "imthanuvnôor". When I am flint-knapping the cares of the world drift away and I form a deep relationship with the obsidian and a chess game ensues. As I chip the obsidian, "sáak", I hear the clink from the hammer stone on the shiny rock and "snap!" the spall, "sakámtaap", flaking off and landing on the pine needle clad soil below my feet. My neck is a bit sore from hunching over my work and I feel the arthritis in my fingers as I grip my knapping tools. I stop and clean my glasses to better see a red headed woodpecker, "chamnúpanach," that has been mocking me from a nearby pine tree, I wonder if he relises his place in the sacred world of the Northwest Indian cultures. I hear the breeze in the trees as the sunlight dances between the branches and needles. Merv George, religious dance leader, "ipeetháran", for the Hupa tribe, says; *Even the trees dance."* Today "ítam" they dance "píhivrin" for me and I chip obsidian, "sáak" and sing, "pákurih", for them! Someone's' old shaggy dog, "tivárarih", wanders into my camp and sniffs around for food scraps, and likewise a small hunting party of large blacks ants, "asvuut". The air is a flying circus of acrobatic insects darting about in the sunlight, "yupxántaak", the shrubs glowing green as the meadow hiding just beyond the trees. The dog wandering off with a slight limp gives a halfhearted bark at a fluffy tail gray squirrel chirping on a pile of pine cone,"úus", fragments. In the distance the babble and crackles sing out from the golden stream, last night it was filled with a symphony of frogs, "xanchíifich", and crickets, "akrahchiripchírip". I pause to take an overall look at the obsidian,"sák'as", spear point, "sáak," I am finding in the stone, but I am interrupted by the high pitched buzz of a hunting mosquito, "chanáakat", and then her familiar sting on my forearm. This morning, "máh'iit", I was bitten by a horse fly, "araramvanyupsítanach", and I scratched the wound until it bled and my fingernails spread red up my lower leg. As I start back at the chess game of knapping at hand and discover I have misplaced one of my knapping tools. I have not gone anywhere interesting or even left the log segment I am setting upon? I look for several minutes; stand up with an avalanche of obsidian dust, check the ground for the falling tool but nothing falls into the soil below? I would retrace my steps but there hasn't been any! Was the dog, "tivárarih", a trickster? Maybe the squirrel, "áxruuh" was up to some hijinks? Was the thief "ánaach", the crow, whom recently and loudly came hopping into the camp, is he the protagonist? In any event the tool has mysteriously disappeared! So I give up and walk over to my tent and retrieve an extra tool I have brought, I keep them numbered for just such an occasion, I can continue flintknapping. I look around the camp on my return to the log seat; I get my tools reorganized where I can easily get to them; pick up the shiny obsidian blade and reevaluate my plan of attack. A few more strategic moves and "checkmate!

Blade Art: Val Waldorf, Crows' Nest Art Studio.

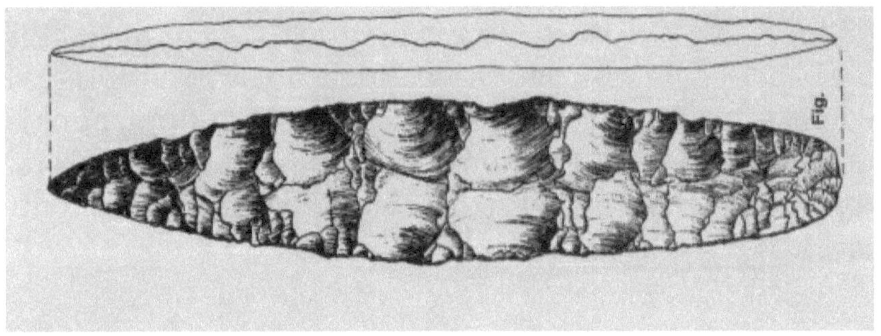

According to Carol Howe (1979); *"the amount of control that a skilled workman can exercise over obsidian is amazing. Theodore Mus-su-peta-nac Orcutt, a Karok Indian, one lived at Red Rock near Dorris, California. He learned the arrowhead maker's art from his father, who was the village specialist. The giant blade in figure 1, now in the Nevada Historical Museum at Reno, Nevada, is an example of his work, though not ancient, it represents the almost lost heritage of an ancient art. Ted Mus-su-peta-nac Orcutt told Alfred Collier of Klamath Falls that it took years of practice for him to become proficient."*

 Theodre Orcutt (1862–1946) King of the Flintknappers: Karuk The Ceremonial Deer Dance KnapperKaruk Master, King of the Flintknappers. at the he turn of the last century there were many flintknappers working at their craft. One of these knappers stands out among the rest as he carried on a sacred tradition, the white deer knapper. The White Deer knapper had the honor of knapping the massive obsidian blades

for the world renewal ceremony known as the White Deer Dance. During this time Orcutt was knapping more than ever and was selling items throughout the eastern United States, Europe and Museums throughout the world. He had well received exhibitions at the California State Fair in Sacramento, and he had shipped his points to many hundreds of museums and collectors. It was in this period also that Ted's ceremonial blades went from the 30 inch long giants to the 48 inch long monsters that made gave him the title "king of the flintknappers". This same time period Ted took a half ton block of glass Mountain obsidian and carefully and precisely knapped a 48 1/2 inch long ceremonial knife, which was 9 inches wide and only 1-3/4 inch thick. This massive biface blade still hold the world record for size, it rested in the Smithsonian Institute, but is missing now. A similar one is in the Nevada Historical Museum at Reno, Nevada. In the Natural History museum in Sacramento there is collection of large Orcutt blades

Rough idea of division of labor this is what I found: flint quarry:

1. (Orcutt= Mussupeta-na.) set up animal traps near perimeter. Coyotes for bounty, others for food.
2. (Uncle=. Mus-sey-peu-ua-fich) or both, collects wood for house and fire, builds a wooden "flint house" to live and work out of at the quarry.
3. (Orcutt,= Mussupeta-na.) goes hunting, food and bounty animals.
4. (Uncle=. Mus-sey-peu-ua-fich) stone cliffs cleaned of dirt to lithic material exposed and fire build against stone.
5. (both)dirt piled on hot stone to heat treat material and hold in the heat.
6. (both) lithic material dugup after cooking and water thrown on large pieces to fragment, (check)
7. Men switch back and forth with firearm guarding for claim jumper, thieves, murders and wild animals.
8. While waiting for flint to cool.
9. When flint cools, men take turns excavating the manageable sized heat treated material. Food prep, firewood collect, flint-knap, pipe carving, wound treatment There are many taboos that have to be adhered to as well, no drinking liquid while knapping. Also, code of ethics must be adhered to.

"As of late many knappers are creating ever larger pieces of lithic art in the form of huge bifaces. Cole Hurst had filled Orcutts shoes in providing ceremonial blades to Deer Dance Obsidian blade bearers. Emery Coons reportedly percussion bifaced a 50 inch preform and managed a 40 inch finished neo-fact. I wrote the Coon's family and requested information and a photo by received no response. At the California knap in this year, large the key-word. Many from other states, such as Coons in Oregon, are also thinking large and obsidian suppliers are selling more mega slabs than ever. Named the Orcutt syndrome after an old time knapper named Ted Orcutt, whom was known for his massive biface work later Don Crabtree came on the scene, perhaps a student of, or witness of Orcutt's knapping. Don worked for Dr. Kroeber and Kroeber had photos graphed and interviewed Orcutt, a Karuk on the Hupa Reservation. "Several of master flintknapper Graig Ratzat's students entered the strange world of the giant obsidian blade knappers. As many of my blog readers know, I am writing a series called "big blade blogs", I have covered Theodore Orcutt, Emory Coons, Cole Hurst and know, Grog Verbeck. Although my fellow Bakersfieldians were acquainted with Grog, I having been out of the loop for quite some time, had never heard of him. It was quite serendipitous; I was on a trip to Anza Borrego desert with my eldest son James , he was returning home to U.C. Davis and gave me ride to a knap in near Sacramento on the way. There in the center ring was Grog Verbeck knapping out very large, monster bifaces. Grog is a long time student of the master knapper, Greg Ratzat of Neolithics fame; in fact he cooks for the class up at Glass Buttes.

Grog Verbeck was raised in the mall town of Staatsburg, on the great Hudson River in New York. He is descendant of the Cherokee tribe by way of his mother's full-blooded great grandmother and his great uncle served on the Osage tribal council. Since Grog was a young boy he had an interest in Indian artifacts and life skills including bow hunting, tanning and fire starting. In college he pursued Native American studies and new world archaeology. He made his first arrowhead as a boy and has been addicted to flintknapping as an art for nearly ten years." Grog knaps boulders and spalls and an occasional giant slab. Grog obtains his lithic material from the glass buttes area of Oregon with his longtime friend and mentor, Greg Ratzat. Grog a chef by trade and runs a private chef service, HeyChef.com, in Lake Tahoe, California. "Hey- Chef!" Began serving Truckee in 1996 and focused on the private chef services of accomplished chef, Grog Verbeck. For more than a decade before landing in Truckee, Chef Grog served in New York as the private chef for Phil Donahue and Marlo Thomas, where he prepared meals for their celebrated dinner guests from the theatre and political worlds, including, Hillary Clinton (Gogslithicart.com

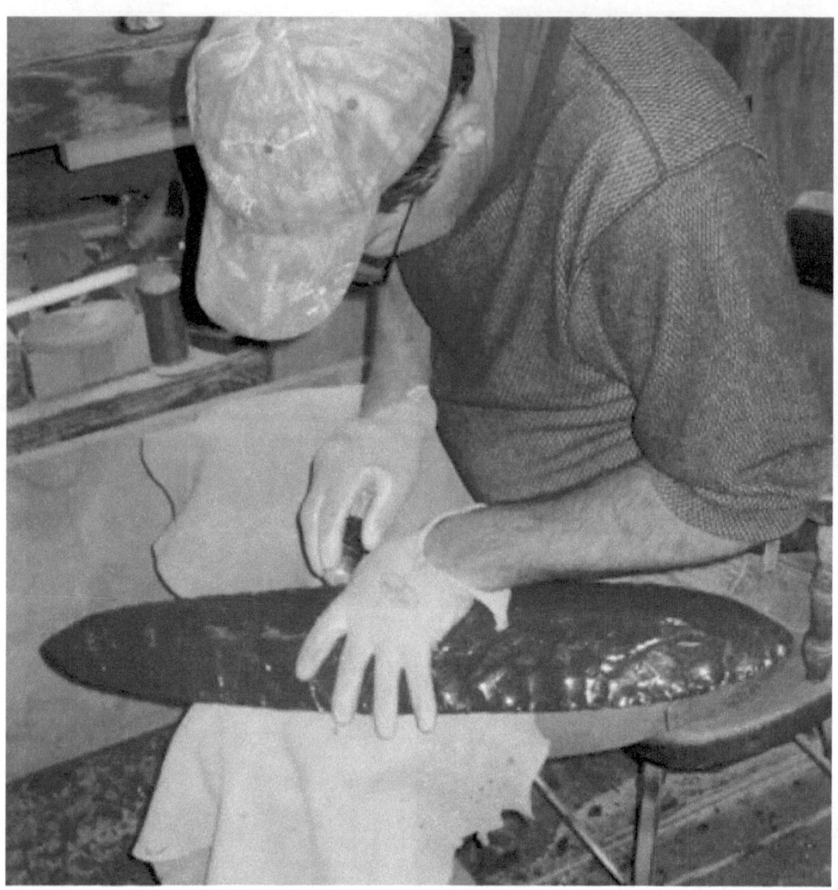

ole Hurst was born October 14th 1960 in Fort Madison, Iowa and within a few years his family moved to East Wenatchee, Washington where he still resides. Growing up he found arrowheads, scrapers and fragments of stone artifacts which sparked his curiosity in how they were made. Cole started flintknapping in the mid 80's when he was in his mid-20s. Cole Hurst didn't know what I was doing, just experimenting. It was in the late 80's that he got a copy of "The art of Flintknapping" by D.C. Waldorf. Then later he met D.C. in 1990 when he was there in East Wenatchee with the Buffalo Museum of Science to take part in one of the digs at the Richey Clovis site, which is only a few miles from where he lives. That is when Cole's knapping really took off. He has made several trips to Glass Buttes to quarry Obsidian; also e has networked with other flintknappers to acquire stone from all over the United States and around the world. Cole bought a rock-saw to conserve on materials as well as a kiln for heat-alteration. 1995 saw the creation of more new knap-ins – Cole Hurst hosted the Wenatchee Knap-in, and the start of the now traditional 'Pot-Luck' Dinner. Community dinners were organized before 1995 but they now became the norm. One only has to attend a single PSK Knap-in to realize what gourmets' knappers (or their spouses) are!

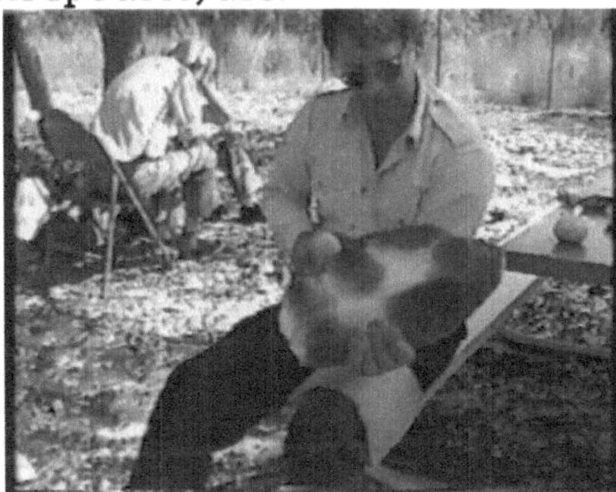

Cole's knap-in further established the commitment to "free instruction". Those with more advanced skills freely tutored those with less, and new techniques and tools were demonstrated and explained. Cole's knap-in also heralded the starter of Paleo Art displays. Where at prior knap-ins folks sometimes brought their points and blades to share, there was a dedicated display area at Cole's. Not only stone points and blades but finished knives, self-bows, and other Paleo Art.

The year 1995 was very significant to Cole and the PSK, several Master Knappers'; Steve Allely, Jim Hopper, D.C. Waldorf and Steve Behrnes all came over and attended the annual Richardson Rock Ranch Knap-in and passed along some 'handy hints'. Later that year, In July1995, the late "Spank Monkey" Dane Martin hosted "a Day with D.C. Waldorf", at his home. D.C. Waldorf not only demonstrated some of his techniques and knapping principles but became a member of the PSK! D.C. Waldorf has influenced thousands, was one of the founding fathers of the Missouri knapping style, work bench pressure. When I was a kid I was very interested in arrowheads. I used to find them once in a while when hunting with my dad and brother. Like many folks dabbling in flintknapping I eventually came upon Waldorf's book, "Art of Flintknapping". The books have sold many thousands of copies and are considered a classic. "The Art of Flintknapping" by D.C. Waldorf has been in print since 1975. Over seventy thousand copies sold. It's come to be known as the Flint Knapper's Bible. If you are interested in learning how to work flint in the same manner as Prehistoric Man, this book is for you. It covers the basics such as tools, raw materials, percussion, pressure and indirect percussion flaking, as well as advanced theory. The new Fifth Edition has been updated with appendices covering the use of modern tools such as copper billets as well as more on antler pressure flakers and was a full 80 page book with over 100 illustrations by world renowned artist, Val Waldorf. According to John Whitaker (2007) "The second edition was much more expanded and improved, with illustrations by Val, who is a trained artist. It also received wider publicity, as Callahan reviewed it favorably in Flintknappers' Exchange (1979)". Errett Callahan conveyed to me (1984) that he coached Val in the specifics of flake stone artifact illustrations. He also stated that he used the Art of Flintknapping as his text book for all of his classes in the 1970s and early 1980s.

At eight years old D.C. Waldorf became interested in Indian traditional technologies. At about fourteen years of age he discovered
a nail could pry flakes from the edge of broken glass and flint
spalls. Later he found that copper and deer tines worked better
for the pressure knapping method. D.C started percussion knapping about 1968 after reading Howell's book "Early Man". H was,
at the time one of only a hand full of knappers on the planet. He
joined the Archaeological Society of Ohio. His point become so
well made that he was banned from selling or displaying them at
the meeting.

D.C. Waldorf uses antler and stone for percussion and copper and
antler for pressure. D.C. and his wife Val took over the "Flintknapping Digest", request, and turned it into "CHIPS" - this was a huge
success. He also wrote many other books, including novels out of
his rural Missouri cabin. D.C. and Val made a good living with
"Mound Builder Books". Later D.C. Waldorf became one of the pi-
oneers of the new Danish Dagger movement. He worked with
other dagger knappers on occasion such as Callahan and Stafford.
PSK Membership and attendance grew by leaps and bounds starting in 1995 and in accelerated in 1996. The Medicine Creek Knap-
in, hosted by Cole Hurst, saw the real beginning of the meaning of
the PSK, whose stated purpose is to '"to serve as a platform from

which to promote and practice knapping basics and skills Cole has held the Wenatchee knap-in since 1995. Cole has chipped different point types found across the U.S. Cole has played with many different styles of knapping. Danish, Egyptian, Mayan Eccentrics, parallel pressure and percussion flaking and Flake over Grinding. Through the 90's his main focus was the Wenatchee style Clovis points. Cole made many and tried several different fluting techniques with pressure jigs, today it is direct percussion fluting. In the mid to late 90's Cole wanted to make larger pieces and began making the large bi-faces, his first deer dance blades. Since that time, the large Clovis points and Ceremonial blades is about 80 percent of Cole's knapping. He has made many up to 16 or 18" and the quest for even larger blades have lured him. Finding material large enough is a quest in itself. Just in the last few years have Cole found pieces up to and beyond 24". Currently Cole is working on a pair of blades that may exceed 28 inches. "Some may think using slabs is kind of cheating, I don't, all big blade knappers agree that slab knapping has its own inherent difficulties it is much harder to get into all the squared edges and fragility. Not to mention, you get more usable material by cutting slabs, more than one centerpiece than by "spalling"- Without slabs hundreds of pounds of obsidian would be wasted, when one boulder can produce one or two giant blades on a good day, if sawn with a diamond saw these precious large pieces can yield dozens of large to giant blades. These giant blades are indeed rare and precious. With many of the lithic sources being considered for National Park status, these quarries will be off limits forever, and the time of the giant blades will end, and their value increase many times over, California has already closed most of their obsidian sources to knappers.

Emory Coons, world record holder for largest biface, was born in Burns Oregon in 1971 and started flintknapping at the age of five, 33 years ago. He has resided in Burns most of his life and attended Burns Union High School winning awards in the crafts department for jewelry two different years. He has been perfecting his skills as a artist ever since, flintknapping, silversmith, lapidary and teaching his craft to others. He has been on OPB on The Caveman at Glass Buttes and Channel 2 News Boise Idaho about the Nyssa rock and gem show multiple times. Several newspaper articles have been written on his art from gem and mineral shows he has attended in Nyssa Oregon, Burns Oregon, Madras Oregon, The Dalles Oregon, Pendleton Oregon, Mission Oregon, Salem Oregon and the Oregonian in Portland Oregon and Golden Dale Washington. The Pendleton Mission papers had a mention for round-up as well as the dozen 18 inch blades he chipped which were built into the Umatilla Veterans' Memorial wall. He has taught classes in flintknapping at Indian Lake for the Umatilla tribe four years also the wild horse atlatl demonstration as well as Pipestone Creek Alberta Canada and in Medicine Hat British Colombia Canada for the Jr. Forest Wardens, at Northern Lights out of Slocan Canada twice, also demonstrated flintknapping along the Oregon Wagon Train in 1993, Baker interruptive center, and Windows to the Past for the BLM and Forest Service. Then there's knapp-ins (arrowhead makers conventions) at Glass Buttes Oregon, Ed Thomas Golden Dale Washington knap-in, Richardson's rock ranch knap-in and the Brad Boughman- Jim Hopper Knapp-in on the upper North Umqua some of the great knappers come to these events to show their skills and teach. Emory attends gem and mineral shows like the Confederated show in Ontario, Nyssa Thunder Egg Days, Prineville Oregon, and Hines Oregon Obsidian Days, a show his father started and the Madras, Oregon gem and mineral show. At these shows he can find most of the exotic materials from other countries, like fire opal from Australia, Brazilian agate, Condor agate from Central America, or crystals, Idaho star garnets and other gems to make arrowheads or Jewelry.

The Fire Obsidian is one of his favorites to find and work. His work can be seen at Boise University (display), Omsi (display), Great Basin Art in Prairie City, Oards 'War Hawk '(tomahawk heads assembled by Great Basin Art), The Edge Company magazine (War Hawks), or some of the local Burns stores. Most of his work has been sought after by private collectors and as gifts. His friend in The Dalles, Jason Hinkle, has oregonthundreggs.com and has put a web page up for Coons Lapidary with pictures and contact information for the selling of his art. Kenny hull a friend of his is a producer and asked him if he knew any big blade makers being he is Emory's x brother-in-law and he taught him how to chip it was nice so Kenny sent him the idea and he chipped the one they wanted and guess Vin Diesel said nope it wouldn't do that one was going on his own personal wall so Emory had to make 2, he only could muster $400.00 each out of Kenny. A 24 incher in movie a 26 incher for Vin's wall.

Vin Diesel (born Mark Sinclair Vincent; July 18, 1967) is an American actor, writer, director, and producer. Emory makes three to four giant blades a year, this since he was 18, he is now 39 years of age. Which is about 54 mega-blades to date. Emory is so good at spalling that people nearly kidnap him to reduce giant boulders. He is getting a 43 pound billet and the late Rick Woodram left him a 6 foot drag saw, so who knows what monsters may be instore!

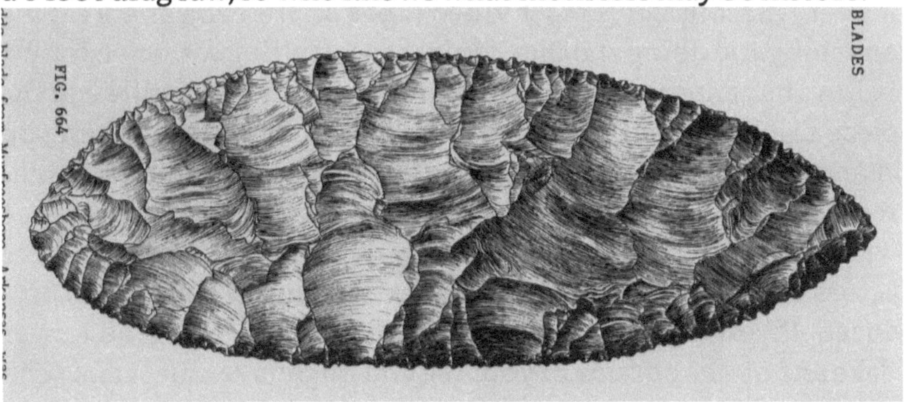

"It's not been easy to make any sort of living being a flintknapper, sure you meet a lot of people, but your still alone in a crowd. Most knappers are either white haired old farts, like Ray Harwood, and choose this as a retirement hobby, not a career. You want to learn from the best to be the best. When no one is there to guide you on angles, edge prep or what material is the best and so on, it's very discouraging. Most video tapes on the subject are saying one thing and doing another, for instance; telling someone to "hit below the centerline" but everything that comes off will keep the piece thick and looking like a speed bump, take note, when you change the degree of hit to that platform it can do many things some of the worst being: put a hinge fracture in it, snap the piece with too much force or occasionally over thin by sending a flake across the piece 1/2 to 3/4 . I tell my students if the edge is produced. If you the set the biface on top your leg, you get a longer flake and on the outside of your leg you might overdue it and send the flake all the way over. It is extremely dangerous procedure to conduct. The main thing is consistency. When I was learning, I was fortunate to be able to watch a couple of the best flintknappers at work, notably, Steve Allely from Oregon, an artist in his own right, and Brian James. Steve used copper and one angle and Brian used mostly horn and stone."

Steve Allely is knapper who began breaking rocks in 1967 and hasn't slowed down much in the last 40 plus odd years of working stone. Although he can make many styles of points and knives, he specializes in beautiful high color points of the Western United States. Steve is also an accomplished flat work artist in painting and illustration. Additionally, he is a bow maker specializing in the subject of Native American archery for over 20 years. He has illustrated a number of books and is published in the well-known Bowyers Bible book series with Jim

Hamm as well as others. As a hunter, he has taken a number of deer with his sinew backed bows obsidian tipped arrows and dressed them out with obsidian knives. World champion close in notching, Steve also replicates various Native American material culture items for museums and interpretive exhibits. He has also taught hundreds of knappers without asking anything in return. When he's not breaking rock, scraping on bows or wielding paint brushes he periodically plays Celtic music and doodles with several kinds of bagpipes. Steve and his wife make their home in central Oregon, a "rock rich" area for a western knapper. Emory Coons and other well-known knapper attribute much of their knowledge to Steve. One hit could be above the centerline later actually at the holding angle it was always below the center line because it moves as you tip the piece; I did not catch on to this variable dynamic right away. You could see what Steve was doing by the angle and platform below the center line. I adapted both of their techniques to work for me and started making larger bifaces. I had never heard of Ted Orcutt before Ray Harwood, of CSUN, sent me an article he had written on the subject. It was never about beating Ted Orcutt's record, I just wanted to make have fun and share things that no one attempted doing. If not for knapping, I would have gone nuts long time ago. It's nice to sit out in the hills watching clouds or a creek knapping a point, thinking of how my ancestors did this out of necessity, rather than going and ordering a Big Mac. One of my proudest moments was when I was given a few arrows my dad killed deer with and I took off the "bent herders steal tips" and put my own obsidian arrowheads them. I took these special arrows out on the hunt into the deep wilderness and was fortunate enough to fell both a cow elk and a forked horn buck. Yeah, I have chipped tons of rock in some pretty weird things, and I've loved every minute. Flintknapping has gotten me through all the rough times in my life and if I couldn't do that anymore I would not have the wherewithal to be typing this for you all.

Errett Callahan was founder and president of the Society of Primitive Technology for many years. The Society is an international organization devoted to the preservation of a wide range of primitive technologies. The SPT preserves and promotes this knowledge principally by means of a remarkable magazine, the Bulletin of Primitive Technology. The one who was supposed to do the marketing dropped out and little became of "Aztecnics". Errett markets his obsidian art through "Piltdown Productions" in Virginia. Callahan is best known for his published work; "The Basics Of Biface Knapping In The Eastern Fluted Point Tradition; A Manual For Flintknappers and Lithic Analysts". This was published in Archaeology of North America. He has also published many other books and articles.

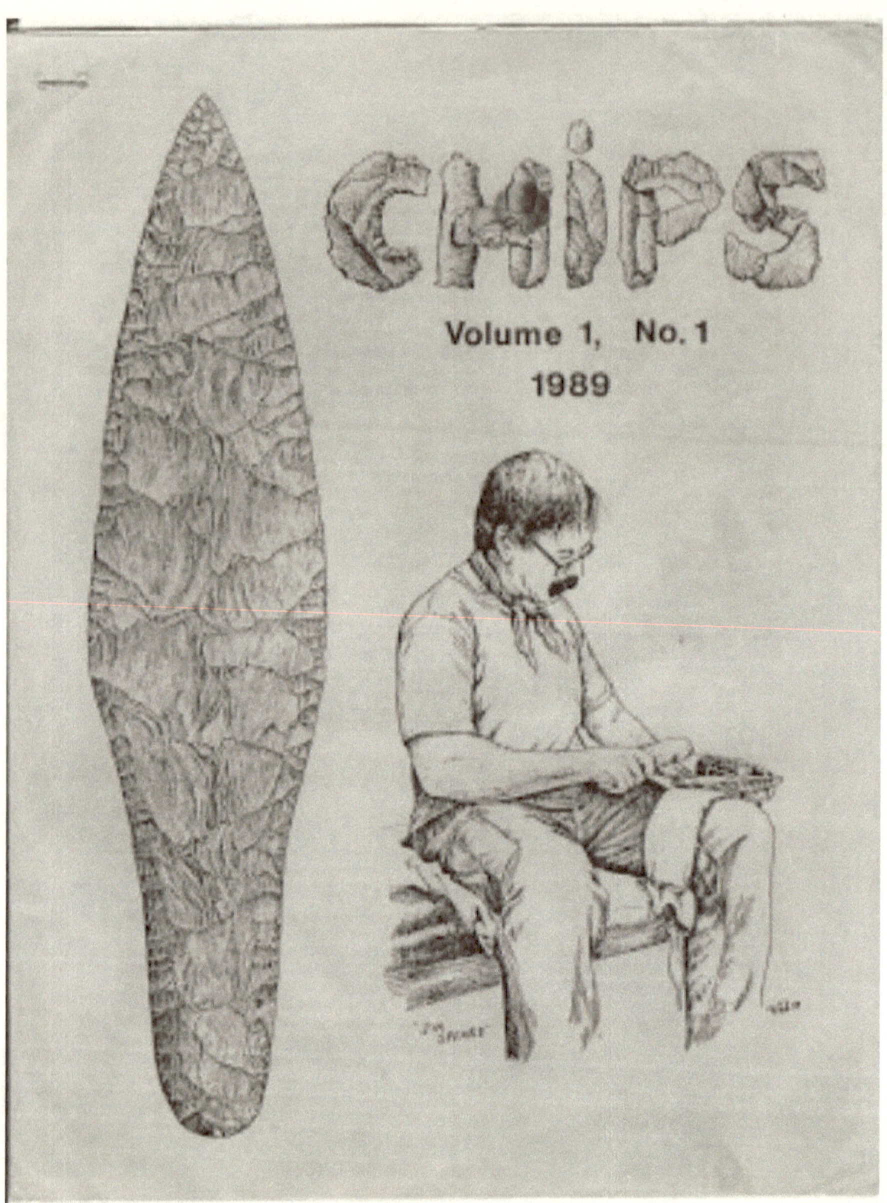
CHiPS
Volume 1,   No. 1
1989

J IM SPEARS has undoubtedly influenced dozens, if not hundreds of knappers. It is difficult to separate the influence of Spears and Waldorf on the knapping world; they are sort of attached at the hip in some respects. Jim Spears, the knapper that pioneered modern theory of isolated platforms for large Cado blade thinning, after many years and many tons of flint he became one of the best flintknappers of all time, his large, thin, patterned percussion blades of colorful flint are masterful and each is a work of art. "Jim pieces" as they are affectionately called by collectors, fetch a handsome price. The largest noviculite point ever made was a `Jim peace" and was 20 inches long, and was made of raw novaculite.

B ob Hunt is a flintknapper who lives in the Kansas City area of Missouri. He helps put on and sponsors the country's largest knap-in each year at Fort Osage near Kansas City, Missouri. He in fact began one of the earliest knap-ins around 1980. As the pictures on this page would suggest, his nickname is "Big Flint". Home at knap-ins Bob Hunt is a fan favorite at Fort Osage, Rocky Hollow, Cahokia Mounds and other famous knap-ins, have undoubtedly run into Bob Hunt, a master of the art of percussion knapping creating giant blades, such as Tennessee swords. Knapper, Phil Love, also creates these swords, but I could not locate him. Bob Hunt has learned alongside the likes of Jim Spears and D.C. Waldorf. In 1979 he met Fred Bollinger at the Cahokia Mounds knap-in. Bob experimented with percussion knapping at Fred's side in 1983 and has been at it ever since , knapping Edwards Plateau chert points up to 25 inches. Bob Hunt used copper bopper technology, which now, it seems may have been used by

Native Americans as well. I met Bob through my old newsletter "Flintknapping Digest" in 1984."

Silicosis is caused by exposure to and inhalation and accumulation of silica dust in the lungs. Its degree of severity appears to be directly related to density, length of exposure, particle size and type of lithic material. The best way to prevent silicosis is to minimize the inhalation of suspended silica dust. The best way to avoid exposure is to knap sparingly or not at all. While knapping, dust avoidances may be accomplished by working outdoors and by wearing a respirator mask, dust masks apparently do not have small enough filtration. Even if you only wear your mask for the more dusty operations, every little bit helps. When working without a mask, try to time your breathing to avoid inhaling the dust. Changing or brushing off your clothes after knapping may also prove useful and will keep the harmful razor sharp particles away from family and pets. Silicosis can be deadly or contribute to other lung ailments and hasten death. I actually keep my knapping close in the back porch and wash them separately from the rest of our clothes. I went to an Indian sweat lodge once after doing knapping obsidian at a pow wow, I could feel the tiny cuts burning in my lungs. Furthermore, I once goy lithic dust up my nose, it got infected and spread to the outer membrane of the inside of my skull. I had to have a hole drilled into my dull and have my massive brain cleaned and sanitized. I had to be on antibiotics for weeks.

Closing: By Jim Keffer and PSK Elders
Ray Harwood has always been a flintknapper, at least as far as he remembers anyway. Flintknapping: The art of making stone tools such as arrowheads, knife blades, spear points, atlatl points, scrapers, etc., by remove flakes from conchodial stone via percussion or pressure flaking. Ray's father dabbled with obsidian (Obsidian: A glass-like rock formed by volcanic activity (volcanic glass)). On occasion and when his brother Ted saw the Crabtree film in college and came home with new enthusiasm, the race was on. Ray began experimenting with additional methods, as he was addicted.

On a trip to northern California the family procured a small load of small obsidian boulders. Ray proceeded to reduce one core but somehow managed to cut off one of his toes. With no medical insurance in the family, Ray's dad sewed the toe back on, it survived but never moved after that.

Ray made extra money selling modern arrowheads and doing minor artifact restoration and replication all through school, having classified ads in many magazines. He attended CSUN where he studied under Clay Singer in the lithics lab at the Northridge Archaeological Research Center.

In 1983 Ray wrote "How to Make Bottle Glass Arrowheads" started the flintknapping newsletter; Flintknapping Digest. Later that year Ray founded the California Flintknapping Rendezvous and the following year started the Wrightwood Knap-In with his longtime friend, Dr. Alton Safford. The Wrightwood Knap In Video was the first or one of the first videos ever sold.

Since the early 1980s Ray has written the self-published book," The History Of Modern Flintknapping" and had dozens of articles published concerning lithics and/or flintknapping. He also helped knapper Gary Pickett with starting the world's longest running monthly knap-in, "The Bakersfield Knap-in" in central California, where he just returned from the 15 year celebration. He also has several knapper blog sites including a fairly popular one at: http://flintknappingmagazine.blogspot.com

Now a member of the PSK Ray has just returned from a visit with Emory Coons in Burns Oregon and the Kettle Falls, Columbia River Knap-in in Eastern Washington. This knap-in hosted by Patrick Farneman (guitar-singer, host of event, wilderness skills, PSK) patrickf@bridgestothepast.org and Kyle Chambers (Kettle Falls Museum - knapper, woodsman at practicalnaturist@gmail.com). At the knap-in he met PSK webmaster Jim Keffer and he states he was truly inspired to rededicate himself to a higher level of flintknapping and to be an active PSK member. Now in Post Falls, Idaho and has been working with Jim Keffer to possibly establish a knap-in the Spokane River area and is working on a new mail order knapping business. He looks forward to meeting and working with PSK members.

The Puget Sound Knappers' Association (PSK) is an informal association of people who enjoy the Ancient Art of Flintknapping. Started in Western Washington, the PSK now has members throughout the Pacific Northwest, Western Canada and several other states and countries. With over 815 active knappers, the PSK hosts a number of major events or 'Knap-ins' a year. We also participate in a number of other events and activities such as Boy Scouts, various Rock Club Shows, School and Museum Demonstrations, Pagan Gatherings and others. The purpose of the PSK and their website is to promote Flintknapping.

FRONT COVER BY VALERIE WALDORF AND HER ART.

VALERIE WALDORF was born September 1, 1954 Valerie Jean Grote spent her early childhood years on her grandparents' farm near Fairfield, Ohio and her teens on a farm her father bought near Greenville. She graduated from Greenville High School in 1972 and married D.C. Waldorf in April of 1974. Together they founded Mound Builder Arts & Trading Co. and Mound Builder

Books. With no formal training in art outside of the few classes in grade school Val developed her talents on her own through constant practice and personal inquiry. Before doing technical illustrations of archeological material she specialized in portraits and wildlife in watercolor and acrylic. She also did stone carving and scrimshaw which sharpened her eye and hand for minute details; this would help her in the pen and ink line drawings of chipped stone artifacts for which she became famous. Because Val had learned flintknapping from her husband in her work illustrating stone tools accurate portrayal of flake scars was everything! In over 25 years, until her untimely death in 2005, she did hundreds of illustrations for books, catalogs, Indian relic magazines, archeological reports, and was the staff artist for CHIPS magazine. In that all too short a time it can be said that Val left us a body of work and a legacy that set the standard for all who would follow her. Val was a good friend, a fellow knapper and the greatest lithic line artist I have ever met. She was generous and kind. An upcoming issue of Journal of Lithic Research is in the works showcasing the Waldorf legacy. Please go to their web site and help support small business. https://www.flintknappingpublications.com